COLLEGE

TO

CORPORATE

*a genuine and lighthearted crash course
for graduates entering the workforce*

Kevin Ratay

Cover design by Erika Duran. Interior design by Butter Designs Books.

Published in the United States of America by Second Serve.

Identifiers:

(Paperback) 979-8-9997256-0-8

(E-Book)   979-8-9997256-1-5

(Hardcover) 979-8-9997256-3-9

To Dad, for providing me with sound advice as I entered the workforce. Especially regarding the 401(k). It changed the course of my financial life.

To Sara, Kevin, and Jon:
This book would likely not exist without you.
The success in my career has your fingerprints all over it.

To Elyssa, who inspired me to write again.
You will always have a piece of my heart.

Thank you.

TABLE OF CONTENTS

INTRODUCTION

A WISE COWORKER once taught me a very valuable lesson: You learn more from losing than from winning.

Whether in sports, schoolwork, or our jobs, winning is a great feeling. However, we tend to learn much more from our mistakes.

Based on that logic, I have learned a *ton* in my career.

From 20 years at five different companies, I'm fortunate to have several positive success stories to share. I've also made mistakes and absorbed learning moments that can probably teach as much or more than the wins.

Recently I began writing down observations and lessons from two decades spent in the corporate world. I realized that the mistakes I've made, as well as those I've witnessed others make, could help college graduates be prepared for what to do and what not to do as they enter the workforce.

A few discussions would soon provide the inspiration to take these blocks of observation and construct them into a book.

Conversations with coworkers as well as with friends in other industries began to reveal a common sentiment: Too often, college graduates are falling short of companies' expectations for their entry-level roles.

A quick scan of the internet supported these claims. Several current articles summarize the surveys, statistics, and concerns that companies want graduates to be better and more prepared for their first year in the workforce.

On the surface it may seem solely like a student issue, yet in this case there is shared accountability. University courses and curricula generally do a good job of teaching specific subject material. However, it's difficult to capture the intangibles of the corporate world inside a classroom or university setting, and it appears colleges also have room for improvement.

My goal with this book is to provide college graduates with a genuine, brief, and informal crash course in the corporate world. The culture and dynamics of today's workplace can present a unique set of challenges for rookies during their first year. If I can create a resource that helps solve this dilemma and develop more prepared graduates, then it should be a win-win proposition for both the company as well as the employee.

Many of the book's lessons are based on mistakes from early in my career. I made plenty of them, and thankfully they became teaching moments and lessons learned. I know I struggled with time management, didn't always play nice with others, and foolishly thought I had all (or at least most) of the answers. I'm also pretty sure I was labeled as a complainer by my first manager, a badge that I probably earned.

I'm confident I would have benefited from a book like this between college and corporate, so hopefully readers can too.

Also, the corporate world can be a serious and regimented environment. Fortunately, most colleagues I've worked closely with also have a fun and sarcastic side, so I attempted to make this an enjoyable read and provide some occasional comedic relief as well. The core content is a collection of over 20 years spent at five different companies – large, medium, and small. The roots are planted firmly in a global Fortune 500 company. They sprawl all the way to a pre-revenue startup with fewer than 100 employees, primarily in customer-facing roles within sales, marketing, and project management.

The lessons are based largely on observations, opinions, and experiences within the corporate world, so that's where the guidance is targeted. As I began to discuss the book with others, they suggested that some of the core content applies to other areas of the workforce such as education and healthcare. If that's the case, let's label that as a positive unintended benefit, and anyone entering the workforce is encouraged to hop aboard and join us for a brief and hopefully helpful ride.

There is a page for notes at the end of the book, so feel free to jot down thoughts as you read through the lessons or even as you encounter applicable situations in your job. I also wanted this book to feel more like a jog or a 5k as opposed to a marathon, so I set my sights on short and sweet.

Thank you for giving this book a shot, and I hope you enjoy the read.

Also thanks to you the reader for making it this far and giving this book a chance. If you found it helpful and enjoyed the read, I would be extremely grateful if you took a moment and submitted a Five-Star Review on the *College to Corporate* Amazon page. Book reviews are especially helpful to both authors and future readers as well.

Thank you!

SYLLABUS DAY

THE 30,000-FOOT VIEW

HUMAN BEINGS AREN'T really meant to sit in meetings or behind a desk all day, with our eyes fixated on a computer screen for nearly half of our lives. At least not yet we aren't.

It's estimated that we have roamed our planet for somewhere between 100,000 and 200,000 years. Office-based jobs have only been around for about 125 to 150 of those, a tiny fraction of our existence.

History shows us that we are explorers, farmers, builders, hunters, and gatherers. However, we find ourselves in the current reality that millions of workers today are desk-bound and WiFi-dependent.

Before digging any deeper, allow me to provide the 30,000-foot view. Yes, there will likely be a bunch of corporate jargon to absorb in your near future. Terms and phrases such as "30,000-foot view," "move the needle," and "let's take that offline" will begin to infiltrate your ears. There are even articles and websites that contain a mini-dictionary full of all the common buzzwords.

We can begin with our own definition, or at least a brief description of the corporate world. The company you work for will likely offer a product or service for sale. It may have 50,000 employees and be publicly traded, or 50 employees and family-owned. The company will have departments such as finance, sales, marketing, supply chain, engineering, human resources, and customer care. Most businesses today are either located in or adjacent to Corporate America, as even small businesses often sell their solutions into larger companies.

If that description seems vague or ambiguous, it would probably be a fair assessment of ambiguity. The corporate world can be a tricky place to describe, whether for a wide-eyed rookie or a wrinkled veteran.

It can be both modern and outdated.

Fluid and stagnant.

Beautiful and repulsive.

Collaborative and lonely.

Rewarding and frustrating.

Learning the various components of the full-time adult workforce takes time and experience. Odds are decent that you're a recent graduate, completing a college education that taught textbook definitions and concepts about your specific major. It probably didn't focus much on the intangible elements of the workforce, which are difficult to teach in a classroom and must be observed and learned over time.

We will cover many of those intangibles, along with other observations and lessons learned along the way. Consider this book a cheat code of sorts, created to put readers a couple levels ahead of others playing the game.

Ultimately, my goal is to inform, prepare, and entertain while shining a light on both the seriousness and silliness that occupy the typical workplace. There are genuine lessons in this book that aim to give readers an advantage over fellow rookies. There is also a fair amount to mock within Corporate America; anyone who says there isn't either is lying or has a reduced sense of humor. So, I'll try to keep it lighthearted and have a laugh or two along the way.

I should also acknowledge that certain chapters contain some cynicism, and could make it appear that I believe the corporate world is a lousy environment in which to work. Overall, it's a pretty good place to make a living. It's a relatively safe way to earn a steady income, fund your weekends away from work, provide healthcare at a reduced cost, eventually support a family, and begin to set yourself up for a comfortable retirement.

Sound a little boring? Yeah, most of the time it is pretty boring. It's a steady stream of meetings, phone calls, emails, spreadsheets, projects, and deadlines.

However, we live in a society where, as an independent adult, it's a survival necessity to make money. Mundane five-day work weeks with consistent paychecks aren't that bad, and they pave the way to enjoyable weekends and a growing 401(k) retirement fund. There are certainly worse alternatives out there.

Together we'll take a panoramic view of the corporate landscape from a mostly clear lens with a small smudge or two on it. Many of the chapters are brief. They are intended to be quick lessons that can be absorbed when read, and then referred to in times of curiosity, especially as you begin to encounter similar situations with a company and its employees.

Also, it would be nearly impossible to learn and implement every single lesson up front, so a fair suggestion would be to select a few that resonate and try to take those along as you begin your corporate journey. You can always come back and revisit the others.

YOUR MOST IMPORTANT JOB

AS A RECENT college graduate, hopefully you have either landed a job or are well along the path of securing employment in the workforce.

Job postings usually highlight a set of roles and responsibilities that align a position with a candidate's education, experience level, or skill set. The job description outlines what is expected in that role at the company, but what is your most important job?

> *Our primary job within the corporate world is simply this: to stay employed.*

Before getting into any specific observations and lessons, it's vital to understand how significant it is to maintain steady employment. Our most important job is to *have* one.

The goal is to stay employed at your current company, earning as many standard paychecks, variable commissions, and any other forms of payment or benefits that are offered to employees in your role. That may seem oversimplified, so to examine it more closely, let's take a brief look down the road of your first job. It will likely produce one of three outcomes: two of them are positive, one of them not so much.

1. Continue in your specific role, receiving these wonderful biweekly deposits in your bank account, until a logical opportunity for advancement arises at this company.

2. Reach the point where some combination of your company, your manager, and your colleagues frustrates you beyond toleration. It drives you to explore the job market, in which you land an interview and ultimately secure employment at another company.

3. Unemployment. Either you quit out of frustration (usually a bad idea), or your company makes the decision that you or your role are no longer required and they terminate your employment.

The goal is to achieve outcome number one or two and avoid number three, especially by quitting without your next job lined up. The corporate world can be tough at times, and if for some reason you realize early on that this company or your specific role are not a good fit, take a deep breath and give it some time.

Looking for a new job while employed is much easier than while out of work. It allows us to compose a more believable story for interviews, instead of trying to explain unemployment so early in a career. While some companies and jobs can definitely suck, most of the time it's better to be working and in a position of strength, rather than out of work and in a position of weakness.

If the frustration continues to grow, resist the urge to quit. Utilize your evenings and weekends to explore other entry-level opportunities in the job market. However, companies are wary of candidates that spend a year or less at each job and then move on. It sticks out like a sore thumb on your resume, so try not to become a "job hopper" right out of the gate.

It's also a good time to highlight an important facet of the corporate world that will help you maintain employment. We are leaving the education-based environment of roughly the last 12 years, and entering a new phase of life with different priorities and keys to success.

In school, it's fair to say that the primary keys to success and getting good grades are book smarts, studying and memorizing material, and test-taking skills. Alternatively, three of the most important contributors to success in the corporate world are people smarts, hard work, and problem-solving skills.

This change represents both a significant shift and an opportunity, especially for hardworking problem-solvers who may have struggled with traditional tests in school. A strong work ethic, connecting with people both professionally and personally, and solving everyday problems are all crucial to operating successfully in the workforce. Improving and mastering those three strengths plays an important role in maintaining employment and achieving success.

Connecting with your coworkers and treating them as fellow humans is especially significant. A brief tale from one of the companies I worked for exhibits how a diminished ability to connect with people and a lack of professionalism can result in some tough consequences.

This company was small yet growing quickly, and had also cultivated a strong internal culture. They hired a savvy new sales rep with a record of industry success, and right away he began producing at a high level, landing new customers at a fast pace. At first, management was touting his performance and revenue numbers. Unfortunately, he was utilizing some shady tactics and also treating colleagues poorly, to the point where a majority of the customer-facing team had grown frustrated with him. A rift began to form.

Both culture and team performance levels were at risk, and the situation warranted quick action. Instead of tolerating this kind of toxic behavior as a trade-off for the sales increase, management decided to fire this new rep. They also addressed the entire sales team following the termination, explained the whole scenario, and earned some respect back from where it may have otherwise started to dwindle.

It was both a difficult decision and a strong display of leadership, showing that how you treat people at work can be of great significance. This rep's sales numbers on paper would have earned him an A in school. However, that self-centered approach can often fail in the workforce.

As we begin to explore more specific content, the next three lessons are essentially the foundation. They are the tortilla of our corporate burrito. We will then add the rice, beans, meat, cheese, and even some guac at the end as we journey through the remaining chapters.

THE BIG THREE

Show Up, Follow Up

I T'S SUCH A simple concept on the surface, yet somehow it can be hard to follow in the corporate world.

> **Show up to work on time, follow up promptly to complete tasks with colleagues and customers, and you'll be ahead of the field right out of the gate.**

It's a reasonable expectation to walk into your company and presume that every person in that office is good at their job. Or at least much better than you because you're new.

I can confirm that's often not the case.

Over 20 years at five different companies, a recurring observation is that many workers have poor time management skills, taking too long to complete tasks or reply to calls and emails. There are so many excellent employees on the corporate landscape, yet naturally there are many average and below-average ones as well.

Showing up every day and completing quality work on time should begin to create a positive impression at the company and with your manager. It will also put you ahead of many fellow rookies and even some of their current employees as well.

Just how far ahead will vary depending on the company, its culture, and also the specific department. Will simply performing the essential tasks on time translate into shining like an all-star? Probably not. However, your department and the company don't need all-stars that grab the spotlight and gain attention with brilliant individual performances.

Companies are composed of people, yet the corporate world is clearly not an individual competition. Most successful businesses employ a team-driven approach and strategy.

A company's rising sales numbers likely aren't due to having a sales team composed fully of all-star reps. The numbers are excellent because the operations team implemented a new service or the engineering team designed an innovative product. The marketing department then connected this solution to the marketplace with the proper customer messaging. Sales effectively executed the strategy and managed relationships in the field, all supported by a strong customer care team to complete the cycle.

The corporate world is a 4 x 400 team relay, not an individual 100-meter dash.

My sales mentor Jon is one of the people mentioned on the dedication page. Early in my career, we operated as a team, as he was the field sales rep in our territory and I was the inside rep on the phones. We worked in tandem for nearly two years, and I'm fortunate that Jon frequently took opportunities to teach and coach best practices. It paved the way for my eventual promotion to field sales rep and managing my own territory.

Jon's coaching and leadership permeate my career and this book, as he taught many of the concepts and strategies that helped me succeed. He likes to teach with analogies to both cooking and sports, and as someone who enjoys both, I found the references relatable and useful.

Comparisons and analogies are often helpful in learning

any kind of new content, and for some reason the corporate world seems to utilize sports analogies frequently. We already encountered one in this chapter from track and field, and now here's one from football that Jon liked to use: blocking and tackling.

A quarterback throwing a touchdown of course puts points on the board and makes the highlight reel. Yet the offensive line probably blocked the defense effectively, giving the quarterback plenty of time to scan the field and find the open receiver, who also gained separation from his defender. There are many key components of the touchdown beyond just the quarterback throwing the ball. Successful teams likely have a skilled quarterback, but they are often built upon other quality areas that don't always gain much attention.

It's similar in the workforce. While a new ad campaign or slogan might gain positive national attention for the company and its CEO, it's the individuals on the marketing team who created and executed the effort.

The company might get an award at the Consumer Electronics Show for an innovative product or design, yet the engineers who did the work behind the scenes are the primary reason the recognition was bestowed.

The persistent execution of the important smaller things doesn't get a lot of attention in the corporate world. It's not the flashy headline-grabbing stuff, but the blocking and tackling are a crucial component to any team or company success. And if we don't show up consistently, we can't block and tackle in the first place.

As I alluded to in our sports analogies, the Show Up, Follow Up mantra applies to team-focused departments such as engineering or marketing. Showing up when expected is especially important since it's hard to solve a puzzle when there are pieces missing frequently. Plus, there are deadlines within each department of every company, so it's always important to show up and complete tasks on time, or else we risk appearing to be a weak link.

It's also evident in a more individual role such as territory sales rep. Making a sale often requires skill and nuance, but it's not possible to achieve sales without sales activities. The number of phone calls per day or customer visits in the field per month are measured at most companies, and it makes sense that the more sales calls we execute and the more effectively we follow up with customers, the more we will succeed.

The specific act of replying and following up both externally to customers and internally to coworkers is one that continues to baffle my closest colleagues and me for over 20 years. Frankly, it's surprising how long some coworkers take to reply to phone calls and emails, especially from those who are supposed to be all on the same team working toward similar goals. At first I thought that it was just confined to the small sample size of companies at which I've worked. However, in speaking with friends and colleagues in multiple industries over time, I'm confident this is a fair representation on a larger scale.

Sometimes it will take two or three days just to receive a reply; other times it can be more than a week, which are both unacceptable. I've been guilty of delayed replies during stretches of time, hopefully catching the pattern early and reprimanding myself to be better in the future.

There is not a set of documented rules on response and reply times across the rest of the corporate landscape. However, one example of a best practice is that all emails and voicemails should be replied to by the end of each business day.

Of course, meetings and late afternoon calls happen, so a practical guideline in that case would be that all replies happen within 24 hours. If a colleague sends you an email at 4:30 in the afternoon that requires some research and insight, a reply by the end of the day isn't always feasible. However, it should be given its due attention with a response the next business day, ideally in the morning.

One consistent example of strong follow-up and response time seems to be within supply chain and logistics, or even the adjacent shipping departments of large corporations. Generally, if you want to witness fast reply times and speedy conflict resolution, check out a logistics company or a corporation's shipping dock. Replies won't be in days or hours, they will be in minutes. It's the nature of the beast as shipment arrivals and coordination of trucks are always time-sensitive and often urgent.

Another component behind the importance of Show Up, Follow Up has to do with our physical absence from work and the challenge it creates for teammates. Whether it's scheduled PTO, taking the day off at the last minute, calling in sick, or routinely showing up late, it affects both coworkers and managers.

The impact in the workforce is different than in college. It didn't matter much to the class or professor if you skipped a class or two, or if I skipped half of my philosophy and theology lectures my entire junior year. In school, it's really just ourselves who are affected. Not showing up for work, especially when it's unplanned, can create problems for your manager and close colleagues. Therefore, make sure to plan PTO with plenty of notice, and try your best not to call off work at the last minute.

Show Up, Follow Up. The more we miss work or don't complete tasks on time, the more we risk annoying and alienating both teammates and managers, which is the opposite of what we want to do.

Make Your Manager's Job Easier

WE COULD JUST as easily flip it and state the inverse. "Don't make your manager's job more difficult."

Either phrasing works, and the reason that both are true is because there's a good chance your manager's job is already challenging and irritating.

> *Reduce the number of problems and issues on your manager's mind, or at least make sure you're not the source of them.*

There will be days in the workforce when your job as an entry-level contributor seems fairly pleasant or at least neutral. There will also be days at work when it seems like your job flat-out sucks. Whether it's in pleasant, neutral, or flat-out-sucks mode, there is usually one constant: Your manager's job is worse. I would wager that a manager's job is more frustrating than the standard entry-level person working on their team a majority of the time. This concept may be difficult to comprehend as a newcomer, and that's understandable. On the surface it can seem like a manager's job is simply to make sure workers do their jobs, all while getting paid more than those same workers. In reality, it's difficult to align several people to get work done in tandem, especially when it's likely a manager already knows how to perform and complete it at a high level. Also, the painstaking reality of management begins to reveal itself and become more evident over time.

Every job carries a set of core responsibilities and activities that one must complete. As an entry-level worker, those activities for which you are responsible have a significant impact on your manager. It could be creating new ideas to market a product, hitting a sales quota, or finding candidates for job openings. The outcome of your role and your team's performance is the number one factor upon which a manager is evaluated.

For starters, make sure that you and your manager determine a good cadence of communication early in your tenure. There should be several teaching and coaching opportunities in the first couple months, as you will be drinking from the proverbial fire hose and learning a lot. Whether it's one-on-one meetings each week, or just being openly available for questions via call, email, or text, establish a logical plan that works for both of you.

Also, be sure to understand your manager's preferred mode of communication. Some don't care and are excellent communicators who will gladly work across calls, emails, text, and internal company messaging such as Teams or Slack. I have worked for managers who want to do it all over the phone, those who prefer text over everything, and multiple variations in between. If there is a manager preference, make sure you are aware and utilize it accordingly.

Speaking of communication, this is probably a decent spot to point out that you may have to interact with managers or members of older generations, and some are stuck in prehistoric email mode. Instead of utilizing fluid group messaging via Slack or Teams, they prefer to load up a new email, add several colleagues, and launch a topic that requires feedback and a steady stream of reply-alls. Resources like Slack and Teams are statistically proven to not only increase efficiency but also drastically reduce email volume that can annoyingly clog up inboxes.

I recently had a colleague say to me, "If you want me to see it, email it to me." Unfortunately, this kind of scenario exists and will likely persist for several more years in the corporate world. Therefore, it's at least helpful to be aware of it and try to exercise patience if you wind up stuck in email mode with any coworkers.

Another factor of management to remember is that most of the work managers delegate to their team is forced upon them from higher up the corporate ladder. Managers aren't just creating random tasks out of thin air to keep their workers busy. Therefore, completing your work properly and on time helps keep your manager and your team in good standing, which is usually a good thing for you too.

The significance of manager sentiment can also be examined by looking at the size of smaller departments within a company. I've managed a team as small as four people and have also been on teams as large as eight direct reports under one manager. Let's say for this example that the average size team under one manager is six people.

As an entry-level individual contributor, you will generally have one core set of professional matters for which you are responsible. A manager has *six*.

You will have one set of personal issues to attend to. A manager has *six* (plus their own at home). Yes, your coworkers will share, and sometimes shout, their personal issues at work to anyone who will listen. In most cases it's a good idea to keep personal matters outside of work, and we'll address that later in the Leave It at Home chapter.

In addition to all of that, a manager has their own work to complete, plus forced collaboration with other departments to lead larger-scale projects for the company. Six different sets of responsibilities and personalities to manage, plus all the other projects and problems that will likely rise up on a weekly basis. Yes, management can most certainly suck. In many cases the only reward is more money, which at the end of the day may not feel like enough to offset all the extra problems, annoyances, and headaches.

The person who hired me at my first corporate job out of college is the previously mentioned Kevin from the dedication page. I was Second Kevin on his team for seven years at the first company where we worked together, and we reunited years later at a different organization for round two.

Kevin has conveyed sage pieces of corporate wisdom to me throughout my career. Approximately five years in, I approached him one day to inform him that when the opportunity arose, I was ready for the next step and would like to be considered for a regional manager position.

I remember his reply vividly: "Think twice about going into management. Field sales rep is one of the best jobs in the company. It's great to move up, but if I were in your position I would consider staying in that role a little longer."

He spoke directly and genuinely, and I could tell he meant it. He also may have realized that I was still a green 28-year-old who was not yet ready to manage and lead a team. Either way, he was probably right on both accounts.

Of course, workers everywhere will continue to earn promotions for management jobs that they enjoy or at least tolerate. A promotion usually represents success in a role and increased compensation, both which are generally good things. The observations and stories above are simply meant to recognize that there are perks to individual contributor roles as well as challenges to the perceived glory of achieving a management position.

One other piece of useful information will be to observe and determine if you work for more of a manager or a leader. Leaders will proactively take you under their wing and provide advice and coaching. Leaders in the corporate world are effective teachers and coaches who mentor the members of their team and help them grow as workers and as people.

On the other hand, a basic manager is a task-oriented box checker that just wants to make sure the required work gets done. They don't take the extra time or go out of their way to coach or teach effectively. These kinds of managers likely qualified for a promotion to management based on success in an individual contributor role, but they don't fit the mold of a teaching or coaching leader. Unfortunately, this scenario is quite common in Corporate America.

It may be tricky to figure out right away if you work for a leader or just a manager, but it should make itself evident in the first three to six months. A fun little exercise is to think back to college or high school, reflecting on teachers and professors from the classroom or coaches from sports teams. Think about the ones who seemed to care more and taught or coached with creativity and passion. Hopefully a couple coaches or teachers are popping into your head right now; they are the leaders. Conversely, those who just made sure your homework was done or yelled more than they coached during practice are more equivalent to basic managers.

Your first manager as a rookie would ideally be more of a leader. If you identify that you're reporting to a basic manager, it's not necessarily an awful thing, and there's no need to panic. You can always seek the guidance and coaching from a colleague on your team or through a company's mentoring program. Good managers don't always need to be leaders; it just helps when they are.

Whether you work for a manager or a leader, it's still incumbent on individual contributors to get the required work done on time. Managers may also request extra help getting a side task done for the team or chipping in on a new project. Try to say yes whenever possible, assuming it's within your scope of work and comfort zone.

Also, don't confuse any of the advice in this chapter with sucking up to your boss. Nobody likes a brown-noser, so there's no need to be one. This is simply doing your job effectively and to expectations.

Make your manager's life easier at work, and it will likely make your life easier too. It probably sounds cliché and lame, yet most of the time it's unavoidably true: Helping your manager simply helps you.

You're Only a Rookie Once

WE HEAR THE term *rookie* used most frequently to describe an athlete's first year in a professional sports league.

In year one, whether you're with a pro sports team or a company, it's generally more acceptable to make mistakes. It applies particularly to situations where lack of knowledge or experience are the culprit, and we do encounter a lot of new situations as rookies still learning on the job.

Take advantage of being a rookie. Ask questions, learn from your mistakes, and take good notes along the way.

As a rookie, it's okay to be inexperienced, not have all the answers, and make mistakes. There's even a term for it: a rookie mistake, normally used to describe a misstep made by a player or worker whose error would be considered acceptable only for someone new to the role.

Some people might think the corporate world is full of ruthless entities that are looking to fire people for any mistake made or error committed. At a majority of companies, that could not be further from the truth.

Most companies despise firing people. It's expensive and time-consuming to recruit new talent, interview candidates, and ultimately find a qualified replacement. Workers don't usually get fired for making a mistake; in fact, it's okay to make mistakes as long as we learn from them and don't repeat them. Mistakes often present themselves as quality learning opportunities to develop and grow.

In addition to learning from mistakes, be sure to observe and take good notes. Listen when others are giving presentations or speaking during team meetings. We have two ears and one mouth; utilize them proportionately, especially in your rookie year. Plus, your colleagues with more experience don't really care what you think or have to say at this point in your career, and rightly so: you're just a rookie – you hardly know anything yet!

Since you are a rookie, it's okay to ask a decent number of questions. Write them down when they randomly pop into your head during the early days of executing your role. That is the time in which you know the *least,* so you should be asking questions the *most.*

Be sure to ask these questions in the proper venues. You don't want to be the person who holds up team meetings with a lot of questions that pertain only to you. Therefore, make sure you carve out time with your manager, your teammates, and other available educational resources within your company.

Seek out a qualified mentor, ideally within your department or office. Even if you don't pair up formally with a mentor, just be sure to maintain a proactive approach. Seek opportunities to gain knowledge and insight from your manager, colleagues, and company. That will pave the way to a strong start within your initial role, and can impress the right people as you take the initiative to learn.

Whether you are in sales or not, go on sales call ride-alongs if your onboarding plan allows for them. It can be helpful in any department to observe how your company's solutions are sold by sales reps and implemented by customers. The lessons learned in the field are an irreplaceable resource and are difficult to replicate in any corporate training sessions.

The good news is that most companies provide plenty of resources and opportunities to learn what's needed to succeed in an entry-level position. They liked you enough to hire you, they are paying you, and they want you to succeed.

It would be an uncomfortable feeling to enter year two of a job and not know how to perform the role to expectations. However, it would be even worse if you put yourself there through lack of focus and execution during your first year.

You're Only a Rookie Once. Use that to your advantage.

That lesson, along with Show Up, Follow Up and Make Your Manager's Job Easier, are the three components of the tortilla that hold our corporate burrito together.

Before we add more specific ingredients, we've reached a good point to insert a lesson that stands on its own. If it were a competition amongst chapters for the most important long-term lesson in the book, our brief 401(k) journey would no doubt be on the podium.

THE ROAD TO RETIREMENT

A 401(κ) JOURNEY

THE IMPORTANCE OF this lesson cannot be overstated. It can only be understated or ignored.

Contribute early and consistently to your company's 401(k). At a minimum, equal the company match, but try to go beyond that. Keep contributing and don't stop until you near retirement.

I realize that for most readers, discussing retirement means we are hopping in a time machine set 40 years into the future, a virtual eternity from now. How *dare* we look four decades ahead, especially when it involves taking money out of the pockets of your 22-year-old self, the "spend and have fun" person, and giving it to this concept of a future 62-year-old "financially stable and retired" person.

My sincere apologies for all of that, as it's usually more fun to spend in the moment than save for the future. However, I'm confident that by age 60, and even by age 40 or 30, once you have some professional miles in your rearview mirror, you won't regret it.

The most important and accessible asset provided within the corporate world, besides the bi-weekly deposits that fund our day-to-day survival, is the 401(k) investment account. The key to setting yourself up for financial security upon retirement begins with the 401(k).

For those unfamiliar with 401(k) plans, I will briefly explain how to invest and legally avoid paying taxes on a good chunk of money for the next 40 years. Let's begin with an efficient description paraphrased from Forbes' website.

> A 401(k) is an employer-sponsored retirement savings plan commonly offered as part of a job benefits package. Employees select a percentage of their salary, subject to annual limitations, and employers often match a portion (usually around 3-4%) of their employees' contributions. The 401(k) account also provides a unique tax advantage. When contributing to a 401(k) plan, taxes are not owed on the money deposited until we access the funds at retirement, when we'll likely be paying a lower tax rate.[1]

That snapshot will satisfy our purposes within these pages, as those are the most relevant points to know. Forbes, Fidelity, Schwab, and countless other financial institutions explain the 401(k) rules and regulations in great detail, so take some time to educate yourself with qualified resources.

---

1. 401(k) plans are common among many investment firms, and you can find descriptions on their websites. This one is paraphrased from Forbes online. "What Is a 401(k)? How Does It Work?" Forbes, updated March 5, 2025, www.forbes.com/advisor/retirement/what-is-401k.

As a corporate rookie, the most important piece of the 401(k) retirement plan is to get started from day one. When you enroll in your company's benefits plan for health insurance, make sure you also enroll in the 401(k) and begin contributing as early as possible. Many companies today automatically enroll new employees in their 401(k), which is an excellent push in the right direction.

The bottom line is that you trim a few bucks off each paycheck before it even gets into your checking account, and then your company gives you some free money on top of that. Additionally, you don't pay taxes on it until you're retired and likely occupy a lower tax bracket.

Every employee should enroll in their 401(k) account. Anyone not contributing is missing out on both free money as well as a proven investment opportunity.

Take advantage of compounding returns and the S&P 500's average annual gains of 8-10% for as long as you can. There's a famous phrase about simply staying invested in the stock market as opposed to trying to time its ups and downs, a feat which is nearly impossible. That phrase is, "It's *time in* the market, not *timing* the market, that matters most."

How much should you contribute? That's entirely up to you. As your unlicensed and under-qualified financial advisor, I would recommend contributing at least 10% of your salary. Some financial advisors would say even more, to max it out all the way to contribution limits. Ten percent is likely somewhere between the bare minimum and maxing it out, and I'm confident it's a fair target.

There aren't many specific conversations from my early 20s that have achieved memory burn status in my brain. However, one of them is sitting at the kitchen table with my dad when I started my first corporate job. We reviewed and discussed the company benefits package, which included a 401(k) and company match. A veteran of the corporate world who grew up without much, he wisely started saving and investing early. Here's how the conversation went:

Dad: This is your 401(k) for retirement savings. You need to select a percentage from your paycheck to contribute and invest. Go ahead and select 10%.

Me: But the company match is a max of 3%. I don't get anything more for going beyond the 3%.

Dad: Yes, you do. You save and invest more money tax-free for your future.

Me: But Dad...

Dad: SELECT. TEN. PERCENT.

Dad was direct and unwavering; he was also correct. Thankfully, that bout was won by unanimous decision in favor of Wise Experienced Dad over Stubborn Uninformed Child. It's not an exaggeration to state that in that moment, he changed the course of my financial life, as I have held steady at 10% for almost my entire career.

As long as you stay within the 401(k) contribution limits, you really can't be guilty of over-contributing. Just don't be guilty of *under*-contributing or starting too late. Should you find yourself struggling to pay the bills and make ends meet, you can always reduce your contribution percentage with no penalty, even though that should be your last resort.

The bottom line is to start early and contribute consistently to your 401(k). There are resources available to explain the different options within your 401(k) even if you don't consider yourself knowledgeable or comfortable with the stock market. When in doubt, there are usually investment funds targeting a specific retirement date that rebalance automatically based on average age and risk tolerance.

We likely won't use much of the knowledge gained from a corporate career past our retirement date. However, we will use and rely on the savings from a 401(k) every year *beyond* our retirement, potentially a period of 20-30 years. Do not count on Social Security alone, as there's evidence supporting the unfortunate scenario that a decade or two from now, it may be a reduced system compared to what it is today.

In addition to pre-tax 401(k) savings, try to save a little post-tax money from each paycheck as well. It's important to build a rainy-day fund, and also to begin saving for down payments on a larger purchase such as a car, condo, or house. It can be a tough balance to strike, but there are plenty of strategies and formulas out there to assist.

Be sure to research them and come up with a plan that works for you and your financial goals.

200-LEVEL COURSEWORK

Discover Your Schedule Spirit Animal

REGARDLESS OF WHAT department your role resides in, you will be responsible for completing a certain amount of work and tasks on your own. Most of those tasks will require an expected level of detail as well as a specific deadline set by your manager, yet the pace and quality of work are largely determined by you.

> *Develop a strategy and schedule to complete your work. Figure out what works best for you and your company, and commit to the plan.*

Are you an energetic early riser who has a bunch of A.M. energy and wants to complete as much work as possible before lunch? Are you a slower starter that will still get things done yet you function better in the middle of the day? Does your company have more meetings in the morning that require you to do the bulk of your individual work in the afternoon?

As a corporate rookie, it's a fair concern that there won't be enough time in the workday or workweek to complete everything your manager and company expect. The national standard for full-time employment is a 40-hour work week. This is mostly accurate, with some exceptions across the corporate world, as the normal entry-level role likely falls in the range of 40-45 hours per week.

In reality, 40 hours is a lot of time, but it can go by quickly and inefficiently if you don't manage it well. The standard work week is plenty of time to complete the required amount of work in most entry-level roles. However, people seem to get thrown off track by a combination of poor time management, distractions, and procrastinating.

Find a schedule groove that works well for you, your company, and of course your manager. Don't allow poor time management to derail your first role in the corporate world. At the top of most managers' list of annoyances is when people miss deadlines on their work. Proper time management can pave the way for both completing your work on time and achieving our goal of making your manager's job easier.

Every company, manager, and employee are of course different, so there really is no set template or secret sauce that reveals how to best manage and complete one's workload. It will vary based on everything from the nature of your specific role to how many meetings your department and company have each week. The key is to discover the blend that works best for you and the colleagues on your team, factoring in the necessary time to complete tasks around the other time commitments such as recurring meetings.

There will likely be a cloud-based calendar where these time commitments are scheduled and you can incorporate your own calls and meetings. If you're a paper-and-pen person who prefers to write important things down on a checklist, that's okay too. Just be sure to have a system that functions well for you and facilitates controlled management of all your duties at work.

Beyond proper time management, there are of course the pitfalls of distractions and procrastination. Yes, the same distractions and sources of procrastination that appear in college life can also rear their head in the corporate world.

When working in an office setting, the distractions include overly talkative coworkers, scanning social media, and the modern workplace's newest fun fixtures such as ping pong tables and video games. These can all slowly and continually destroy valuable time for productivity within the workday. The list is different and more expansive in hybrid roles working from home, and we'll tackle that in depth during the Remote Control chapter.

It's impossible to avoid every single distraction, and we are all prone to occasional procrastination. Just be sure to keep them as the exception and not the rule.

It's also worth mentioning that there are some entry-level jobs – investment banking is one example – that are infamous for putting recent college graduates through brutal 65- to 70-hour workweeks. This element is widely known going in, and those roles are often compensated nicely while being required to work long hours. However, they do know what they're getting into from the start, so it's difficult to complain about that facet.

For most jobs, if you're able to achieve proper scheduling and time management, the 40- to 45-hour workweek is enough to succeed in an entry-level role.

No Complaints Without Solutions

THE COMPANY YOU work for, as well as your specific role itself, will likely have a well-defined set of processes and protocols. Some of these will be logical and make sense; others will be misguided and confusing.

Whether they are outdated guidelines in dire need of modernizing, or just the result of poor decisions made by management, there are usually a few headscratchers that could warrant a complaint at most corporations.

> **Don't raise a complaint without having a suggestion to resolve it. If you have a complaint, don't voice it until you find a potential solution to accompany it.**

It's very possible that you are in possession of a complaint that's accurate and also features evidence to support its validity. However, it's doubtful that the complaint is original, and it's likely that your manager has already heard a similar gripe before. A complaint like this, especially without a potential solution accompanying it, is an empty complaint.

Managers often grow tired of empty complaints and become annoyed with the complainer as well. There are frustrating elements within many companies that seem backward and worthy of complaint. It may just be some kind of tedious yet necessary process for doing business at that company or in that industry.

Resist the temptation to complain. Early on in my career, it's fair to say that I was more of a complainer than a solutions provider. As a rookie, it can be difficult to keep those complaints bottled up or to designate one from a healthy suggestion or potential solution.

So what should you do if you find yourself with one of these persistent issues or frustrations rising to a boiling point? Take the pot off the burner for a minute. Brainstorm and try to think of a solution to solve the issue. Conduct some basic research on your own and, if needed, speak with a trusted colleague on your team. Challenge yourself to find a realistic solution or at least think of a suggestion to pair with your whine.

If the complaint happens to be unique, legit, and one worth solving, then don't just toss it on the list with the other gripes. Put some time and effort into developing a potential resolution to the issue at hand before you launch that complaint.

Another component of this lesson is a concept that my sales mentor Jon taught me early in my career. He frequently taught using analogies and phrases, and one of his favorite ones to coach with is, "Is the juice worth the squeeze?"

He applied it directly to two areas that we encountered: in calculating the potential payoff with sales activities and strategies, and in voicing complaints up the corporate ladder. In either case, be sure to determine if the goal to achieve or problem to solve is worth the effort, energy, and risk, or if it's not significant enough and is better left alone. I've found it to be good advice on both accounts.

Overall, this lesson's primary takeaway is to practice critical thinking and challenge yourself to create a potential solution before voicing a complaint. If you can't come up with one, it's no big deal; just keep the complaint to yourself for now. Worst case scenario, you avoid being labeled as a complainer. You can always present the issue and a potential solution at a later date if you think of one, and perhaps even receive some positive recognition if it gets implemented.

Complaining often reeks of deflected accountability and a poor attitude, being able to only focus on the negatives and not see the positives. This is not the kind of scent we want to emit in the corporate world.

GIVE CREDIT, ACCEPT BLAME

THROUGHOUT OUR CAREERS, hopefully most of us will enjoy a healthy share of achievement and success. On the other hand, we will also likely face challenging situations in which a mistake is made, or a decision turns out to be wrong.

One piece of advice that aims to address both kinds of situations is as follows:

> *When you achieve success and receive praise at work, accept it with grace and give credit where credit is due. When you make a mistake, hold yourself accountable and don't deflect blame.*

Let's begin on the positive half with credit. Companies give individual credit to their employees in various ways, such as verbal recognition at an internal meeting, through company-wide communication, or even with monthly and annual awards.

Resist the temptation to keep the credit solely for yourself, and don't bask in the spotlight. Celebrate your individual praise or success as a team victory, and whenever possible say "we" instead of "I." It's nice to be recognized, but individual credit is often part of a larger group's success.

Acknowledge any people on your team or colleagues in other departments who also contributed to the accomplishment for which you are being recognized. Even if it's just one or two other people, there will likely be a couple coworkers who fit that category. It's an honor for a rookie to be recognized for quality work; it would be even more impressive for that rookie to acknowledge their teammates' role in the success.

We can explore a few different departments for meaningful examples. Within sales, reps are rewarded with monthly or quarterly commission checks, and also given annual awards for their revenue growth and sales results. Salespeople get to keep the commission check, but they should still give credit to others on their team or at the company. There are likely a few colleagues, whether it's customer care, technical support, or of course a direct manager, who assisted in exceeding individual sales goals.

For other departments, such as marketing, finance, or engineering, team-focused goals are usually the prize as opposed to something like individual sales targets. Managers or team leads often receive the credit; however, if you happen to be singled out as a key individual contributor within a team or a project, remember to share the spotlight and recognize any specific people who assisted with your portion. I'm confident that most individual recognition at companies is also reflective of additional contributions from other colleagues, so remember to share the wealth.

Be sure to recognize these coworkers and thank them accordingly, either verbally or in writing, whichever feels more appropriate given the situation. We don't always get a chance to address the right people verbally in a meeting, yet sometimes a phone call to thank them can go a long way and also carry more meaning than sending a quick email, text, or Slack.

When good things happen and success is achieved, there is often credit and praise to be distributed. When failure happens or mistakes are made, the associated buzzwords are accountability and blame.

One of the primary keys to handling a situation in which you are at fault is to practice accountability and accept blame for mistakes. If you made an error or an incorrect decision, acknowledge the mistake and don't try to deflect it on other people, as that has the potential to backfire.

In addition, contemplate and prepare a response as to what could be done differently in the future to avoid making the same mistake. There's a level of presumed maturity and wisdom that comes from both recognizing mistakes and learning from them. Point out the areas of improvement in what you might do differently in a similar situation down the road.

If you do find yourself in a scenario where you are being blamed for something that was not your fault, there is a proper way to handle that, and it's not in a public forum. If you are blamed in email or writing, consult your manager or teammates first before hitting that dreaded reply-all button.

If you find yourself the recipient of some errant blame at an internal meeting, especially when confident you're not at fault, pause and take the high road. Resist the urge to point fingers, even if they are pointed accurately at the guilty culprits.

You have the right to defend yourself, but first confirm the facts and then construct your reply carefully. Instead of firing right back, say something like, "I'd like to first reconvene with my team or my manager, and make sure we have all the details in line before we proceed any further."

You can likely form the best and most appropriate response when stepping back from the potentially heated or emotional situation and consulting others first.

TAKE THE HIGH ROAD

THIS CHAPTER COULD probably go on forever. It could feature countless stories and tales of corporate colleagues choosing the shady or sneaky route to try and achieve a promotion or some other kind of personal glory. However, considering the 5k-over-marathon approach, I'll at least attempt short and sweet.

Taking the high road would be a simple universal approach to implement if everyone recognized and adopted it. Yet in the corporate world and along with many other lines of work, it's the people around you that make taking the high road a significant challenge.

Let's begin with a basic definition to put us on equal footing.

> *Taking the High Road is choosing the honorable course of action, even when it might be easier to act in a selfish or shady way to take advantage of a situation.*

If we all adopted the golden rule and treated each other the way we wished to be treated, we'd have a much different corporate landscape, and a much different society as well. We live in a world where people occasionally say one thing then do the other, sacrificing other people's well-being for their own.

It's likely that you will encounter coworkers who make self-centered decisions, take advantage of other people for their own gain, and jump on the heads of coworkers to bounce up to the next level. I do not recommend these actions on the corporate landscape.

Treat your coworkers with a fair amount of respect. Try to remember that when you break it all down, they're just a different version of you. They are there to support their life by earning an income at the very same company. When in doubt, treat them as you would want to be treated. It will no doubt be tough at times, but I'm confident it's the best and most universally achievable approach.

Don't screw over a colleague for your own personal gain. People talk within companies, and if you try this tactic, you are far more likely to alienate people on your team and in other departments. It's just poor form, especially on the entry-level scene. It's not more tolerable when done at higher executive levels, but in that arena of inflated ego, authority, and leverage, it certainly is more frequent and expected.

On the contrary, try to assist your teammates when opportunities arise and you have the knowledge and bandwidth. Specifically – and yes, a *little* bit selfishly – assist the ones who you know or think would assist you back. It shows willingness to help others, and as a side perk, accumulating some favors and IOUs can help in future situations.

Additionally, one of the most important High Road lessons I learned early on has to do with winning and losing. Early in my career there were levels of sales success as well as some adversity, yet I was not entirely prepared to handle either. I received some solid advice from colleagues at the time on this topic:

When you lose, say a little.
When you win, say less.

It has a couple different meanings and applications, so let's begin with the adversity. Whether it's a missed deadline on a finance project or a bad quarter in sales, you will likely face questions from management. If you find yourself in a situation that requires addressing them, simply summarize what went wrong, what you learned, and how things can be improved next time. Nobody, especially management, wants to hear excuses, apologies, or finger-pointing.

When you win, say even less. Nobody wants to hear the excuses from adversity, and nobody wants to hear obnoxious gloating or self-promotion either. Whether you create an innovative engineering process or successfully implement a new marketing campaign, don't seek the spotlight or reach for recognition. If it's warranted, it will come, and if it doesn't, let it roll off your back. The people on your team and your manager likely know you were central to the success, and that's usually what matters most.

REMEMBER YOUR WHY

A S YOUR DAYS in the workforce turn to weeks and months, you will likely notice that some of your colleagues are naturally inspired by their industry, company, or specific field of work. They exist at every company, and that level of genuine inspiration will frequently produce high-quality work all while making it seem easy the whole time.

Sometimes it can be difficult to show up with a smile and be fully engaged if you don't possess that natural passion and inspiration. However, it's important to stay engaged with work and your colleagues even during challenging or frustrating times.

Indifference and lack of enthusiasm are not good signals to send, and they can be difficult to disguise.

There's a little trick to achieve or at least emulate this level of engagement at work. Let's call it a strategic shortcut, and those who implement it effectively can appear passionate and stay more engaged.

> *Identify the people and activities in your life that you care about most— the reasons why you work for an income—and channel that passion and energy within your role.*

We can pause for a brief smirk of judgment on this one. I'm pretty sure I reacted similarly the first time I heard of this concept. Yet the corporate world is not a binary situation in which you either do or don't care about the specific company and role in which you work. There are varying levels of passion and engagement, and you can control your approach and adjust these levels regarding your overall attitude toward work.

Remembering your why can help produce better results and also create more meaning in your role, especially one that may be growing tired and weary. When implemented genuinely and correctly, it can help steady the boat when the corporate waves get a little choppy.

Its origin requires a brief backstory from when I was managing a territory over a decade ago. Our company was coming off the heels of a product line that was underperforming our competition in a noticeable way. It was a recurring complaint from our customers, a topic that was dominating internal discussions, and not surprisingly had a negative impact on both our sales numbers and overall psyche.

The answer to our problems had now arrived at our fingertips: a new featured product line that was not only equaling or exceeding expectations, but was beginning to win back business that had started leaking to our competitors.

So what happened just three months into the successful product launch? Inventory mismanagement, resulting in a product shortage and an inconvenient back-order situation for our customers. Frustrating, to say the least.

It was crisis time, and our newly found positive spirits began to diminish. Our manager noticed that our team was a combination of frustrated and deflated, raising concern that we wouldn't deliver results to expectations. He delivered a genuine declaration to our team that went something like this:

There are gonna be challenges at every workplace, and it's how we respond to these challenges that will determine our success. The product and inventory issues suck, and it's easy to be frustrated with our company and its people right now. I'm frustrated with our company and its people right now. At the end of the day, we all have pretty decent jobs, and I want us to remember why we work...what our jobs and our paychecks ultimately mean. The ability to lead the lives you want and provide for yourself and your families. We briefly saw the light with this new product's success. Let's stay strong, keep our heads high, and I'm confident we'll be out of the tunnel soon.

Was it a little corny? Maybe. But it was also accurate and even a little inspiring. I hadn't been in a locker room since high school sports, but at that moment I felt like a coach was speaking and not a corporate manager. He recognized the issues, reminded us that we are indeed in this together, and provided an intangible resource we could utilize.

I imagine this exercise tugged at the heartstrings a little more effectively for colleagues with spouses and especially those with children. I was in my 20s and single, possessing fewer familial reasons for persevering through difficult times at work, so I turned to hobbies and activities.

I preferred experiences over possessions, so I spent my money on vacations with friends, great seats to concerts, and weekend golf.

Are your preferences more tangible? All good, no judgment here. Select an expensive item you either just bought or one you currently desire. Make that the center point of channeling personal passion into a place that currently frustrates you for several hours per week.

Is the Remember Your Why mantra a little bit of glass-half-full, optimistic thinking? Possibly. Yet when we face frustrating situations at work caused by decisions largely out of our control, it can be difficult to stay engaged with your company and your role.

Every little bit can help regain focus and fall back into a good groove. Corporate culture is infectious and can spread quickly, both positive and negative. When the negative vibe strikes a company, things can get frustrating and nobody is safe from it.

It's natural and understandable to go through frustrating periods in which work is viewed as nothing more than an empty transactional agreement, trading your time and effort for money in return. Regardless of how frustrating a situation gets at work, we can always control our attitude and effort. Utilizing a proactive, positive approach is usually better than the alternative of being a negative complainer who emits the "I don't care" vibe.

We never want to show coworkers or managers that we don't care, as it's not a good look and is a tough one to recover from.

PERSONAL & PERSONNEL

HR IS NOT THE COMPLAINT DEPARTMENT

AS A CORPORATE rookie, it's common and understandable to think that the human resources department is the proper place to bring your workplace problems, conflicts, and complaints. Unfortunately, that perception is largely inaccurate.

At most companies, human resources conducts and manages three primary functions:

1. Manage the personnel life cycle and people development

2. Administer payroll and benefits for employees

3. Manage disciplinary actions and protect the interests of the company.

Those functions are three significant components of any successful business. Our colleagues in human resources serve an important purpose, but that purpose is not to resolve minor employee conflicts and issues. It also shouldn't be to babysit coworkers or resolve petty complaints about a manager.

Their primary functions are specific and necessary, as HR occupies a role that can be both challenging and frustrating.

First off, HR coordinates the entire personnel lifecycle at a company. Conception takes place with the recruiting process, finding and screening a pool of qualified candidates for hiring managers to interview for open positions. They conduct the onboarding process for new hires as well as monitor the overall staff performance, development, and culture within a company. HR then occupies the necessary yet difficult role of corporate funeral director when an employee is either terminated or leaves the company on their own.

Human resources also administers the payroll and benefits processes. Benefits season in particular can be a long and arduous process, usually aligning loosely with the NFL regular season. It starts in September, runs all the way into December, and often leaks into January with follow-up questions on insurance plans for the new calendar year.

The third primary responsibility is to manage disciplinary actions and protect the interests of the company. There are potential legal implications that stem from both employee terminations and personnel issues within the existing workplace, so human resources and company attorneys often work closely together. Those discussions usually involve HR managing the process by determining not only the employee's rights, but also working with the attorneys to minimize the negative legal impact to the company.

So what does all this mean for employees outside of human resources? Essentially it serves as a basic PSA and a reminder to manage interactions with HR appropriately. We should be engaged with HR at onboarding, during benefits season, exploring a formal company development plan or even a promotion, and that should be about it.

It's likely that you'll encounter basic problems and challenges at work, with either the company's processes, its people, or both. There are many better alternatives to resolving these challenges than taking them to HR. It's probably not going to produce the theoretically desired outcome from inside our mind's perception, and frankly they are already too busy with their primary functions. They probably don't want to hear it, so you shouldn't be speaking to them about it if it's not absolutely necessary.

If you're having a problem with a colleague, try having a casual conversation with that person to resolve the issue amicably. If the situation continues to escalate, then the next step might be to involve management. Most managers prefer the opportunity to address issues with their direct reports before HR gets involved. They generally do not appreciate it when the first time they are hearing about an issue on their team comes from human resources.

Standard workplace conflict and personality clashes should stay within the specific teams and under those specific managers. HR is not the company complaint department. The inconvenience and annoyance you would be creating for your boss by going around them with a basic issue is usually not worth it.

A footnote to the HR discussion is a quick disclosure that is probably already known: I have never been employed within a human resources department. Most thoughts and opinions in this chapter stem from HR-adjacent experiences and casual discussions with colleagues, including some who held roles in that department.

Based on those experiences and conversations, I'm confident in the general accuracy of this summary on HR and its unique role on the corporate landscape.

Leave it at Home

ONE OF THE more interesting intangibles that employees will face is learning how to manage the intersection of our work lives and our personal lives.

We are all human with a range of emotions, and when we experience good times and achieve victories, it's natural to spread the news to both friends and coworkers. That sentiment can be perfectly fine and even healthy to a certain extent. However, when we experience tough times and challenges, it's even more important to manage those appropriately in relation to workplace carryover.

All of us are likely dealing with some kind of physical or emotional challenge in our personal lives, and those battles are usually best kept away from work.

Personal issues should largely remain in our personal lives. It's usually best to leave those at home and address them outside of work.

The primary takeaway is that in most cases, we should make a proactive attempt to compartmentalize. It's not that we should ignore the challenges in our personal lives, it's just that we should address and discuss these challenges on personal time and not at work.

When we bring issues from home into work, there are several unnecessary risks and potential consequences. First off, you probably don't want to be the coworker who is known for continually complaining about their family, financial woes, or dating life. It can be obnoxious and disruptive to a team's culture or even an entire office.

A greater concern pertains to the actual severity and impact of the specific challenges we are facing. One facet that is easy to overlook when issues swell up in our personal lives is that comparatively, they just may not be that significant or painful. As we mentioned earlier, everyone is likely going through *some*thing, and we often have no idea what that is.

Whether somebody keeps issues close to the vest or overshares to anyone with a set of ears is a decision left up to each individual. Unfortunately, the blast radius of sharing personal situations or struggles in the workplace can be severe and wide. The fact that we don't know what pesters or plagues our colleagues' personal lives should be enough to hit the pause button on bringing personal problems to work.

Your minor gripe about past-due rent this month could make a colleague ponder their mounting credit card debt.

Your fight with a significant other could remind a coworker about their pending divorce.

Your lingering cold could pale in comparison to a private battle with a chronic illness or disease.

Try to compartmentalize any thoughts or problems you may be experiencing and confine them as best you can to your personal life. It's not easy to do, but it's usually worth the effort. When you find yourself wondering whether to share something with coworkers, hit pause and consult a close friend or family member for additional insight.

One exception to this lesson would be a health concern or affliction that will impact your performance at work. In these kinds of situations, there's a case to be made to inform your manager and human resources. Most companies want to know something like that and will work with you to overcome the health situation as best they can. Other than that, it's usually best to leave the less severe personal issues at home.

There is one personal element that is particularly important to keep distanced from the company: your dating life, and more candidly, your sex life. For better or worse, I can speak to this topic from both a position of experience and regret!

Depending on the company and your role, you may find yourself at an office happy hour or evening work function. There may even be complimentary alcohol, which usually doesn't help stay the course on this lesson. Whether it's a national meeting or a random corporate event, these situations can be a combination of fun, challenging, and confusing, especially for warm-blooded humans in their early 20s. Unfortunately, it was all of those and more for me.

In the first month of a job I had just started, we had a national meeting and a new product launch where nearly the entire company flew to our headquarters. On the way to the airport, another new employee and I received some great advice from our manager at the time. It went something like this:

There's gonna be about 200 of our coworkers at this kickoff party tonight, along with live music and free alcohol. It's okay to have a couple drinks and a fun time, but there are two important things to remember. First, don't drink too much and get drunk. And the second is... keep it in your pants!

I listened to the advice, casually smirking while nodding in agreement.

Did I *apply* the advice at the kickoff party that evening? Absolutely not.

I drank just enough confidence juice to turn a fun conversation with a nice single woman from a different department into something more. We hit it off, one thing led to another, and just like that I spurned my manager's sound advice.

Talk about a short-sighted decision and an uncomfortable situation. During the meeting's various sessions the next two days, I should have been focused on learning the material as well as meeting my new colleagues. Instead, my mind was occupied perpetually with all the wrong thoughts.

What do we say when we see each other today? What if my manager finds out? Could we be in trouble? I was uncomfortable, nervous, and distracted, the opposite of what I should have been, especially as a corporate rookie.

This was slowly gaining momentum in the wrong direction, and it was a poor decision especially since I received the proper advice in advance.

We're only human and we make mistakes, making decisions in the moment that end up with outcomes we regret. It's okay to make a mistake and learn from it. However, this felt particularly bad since I was warned, and because I knew it could negatively impact my image and reputation within the company.

There are plenty of fish outside your own corporate pond, so it's usually best to find another lake or ocean.

POLITICS, RELIGION, AND THE WEATHER

BESIDES THE REQUIRED shoptalk within companies, you will likely find yourself connecting with coworkers and speaking about topics other than your jobs. It's inevitable that the conversation between people situated near each other for several hours per week will stretch beyond the spectrum of work.

While the majority of time spent at our jobs will be and should be focused on work, we are also human beings and not robots. There is occasional downtime during most workdays, ranging from quick, isolated chats to discussions over lunch. In addition, a variety of small talk topics can arise during customer-facing meetings with your company's clients.

Of all the potential topics to discuss with colleagues and customers, I'm confident that employees in most work environments should avoid politics, religion, and the weather.

We can begin with the simple and sterile one: the weather. It should be avoided as a topic of conversation for one simple reason: it's boring.

> *Don't talk about the weather. It's mundane, it's known, and it's the same for everyone around you. Challenge yourself to discuss more interesting topics than the weather.*

No one can be offended or angered by the topic of weather in the way that religion or politics can accomplish. However, there seems to be this underlying safety net of filling the air with discussions on the current weather, both internally with colleagues and externally with customers. It's simply not an interesting or engaging subject of conversation.

"Oh hey there Bill, how about that cold weather we're having today. It sure is brisk!"

Or a personal favorite from visiting customers' offices: "Just look at that warm sunshine outside. Bet you'd rather be out there than in here, ha ha!"

Maybe not boring, yet certainly not interesting or engaging. By its universal and predictable nature, the weather simply doesn't have much capacity to be intriguing.

One brief customer-facing example can hopefully highlight this position on the weather as an inferior topic. Imagine that a customer has meetings with sales reps from three different vendors. Upon arrival, two of those reps talk about the weather, and the third rep asks about the customer's town and any local restaurant recommendations. Which one has the potential to evolve into a more interesting and engaging topic as a precursor to the true purpose of the meeting?

It's an easy victory for asking about the town and restaurant recommendations over the weather. For years it has been one of my favorite conversation starters when traveling as a sales rep. Simply open the discussion with something like, "So I'll be staying in town for dinner tonight and want to find a good spot...I usually try to eat local and avoid the large chains. Do you have any good restaurants in the area that you would recommend?"

For the same reason that good sales reps ask a lot of open-ended questions, the neighborhood restaurant discussion usually evokes thought, insight, and interest from the question's recipient. Think about when someone asks you about your favorite local restaurants. You probably perk up with thoughts of one or two great places right away, evoking positive memories of a great dining experience.

For those who see customers on a regular basis, likely in a sales or field marketing role, there's also a potential perk to the local restaurant topic: It can open up a great opportunity to have dinner with your customers. On more than one occasion, the customer has playfully said something like, "Well hey, where's my invitation?!" or "I've got plans tonight so you're lucky I can't make it!"

It opens the door comfortably to a reply of, "I would much prefer the company as opposed to eating alone. How about next time I come to town we make plans to meet for dinner?"

As a result, your next appointment is tentatively booked, and even better, it's a dinner. A significant portion of business and specifically sales is based on relationships and people, and there aren't many better ways to build upon a customer relationship than with casual conversation over dinner.

The local dinner spot is just one topic of conversation besides the weather, and there are many more. From favorite hobbies and TV shows to local sports teams and events in the community, I'm confident those discussions carry more interest and engagement than the weather.

Now that we've explored avoiding the weather, it's time to focus on the spicy ones: politics and religion.

Keep politics and religion to yourself. And if a colleague brings them up at work, avoid joining the conversation.

There is simply far more to be lost than gained when venturing down the winding road of political and religious discussions. They are both so personal and subjective that they often invoke feelings of disapproval and distance when two people disagree on those topics.

Want to put up an invisible barrier between yourself and a coworker or customer? Openly discuss and disagree with a religious or political stance.

It's also shocking that people utilize business forums online to publicize their personal beliefs, especially political ones. I don't understand how essentially putting a name tag on your shirt that says, "Hi, I'd like to alienate about half of you" is good for your business or your personal brand in any industry.

Much more harm than good can result from it, so try not to post and don't comment on other religious or political posts either.

Politics, religion, and the weather: for different reasons, simply avoid these topics as much as you can in any workplace setting.

300-LEVEL COURSEWORK

READ THE ROOM

ONE OF THE more interesting intangibles within the corporate world is the ability to read the room. This can be a difficult skill to both teach and learn, but if you possess the innate ability then it may come easily. If it's not a skill you have acquired yet, then hopefully this lesson will at least help convey its relevance and solicit a desire to add it to your repertoire.

It's worth noting that many of these chapters have a balanced combo of explanations and examples, with a few paragraphs of detail and description followed by a brief story to showcase the lesson. This chapter might be the exception. I'll not only include a bonus second tale from the corporate world, I'll also be light on description as I believe these two stories can highlight the importance of reading the room better than I can explain it.

Before story time begins, I should at least provide a quick glance of what reading the room means in a corporate setting. At its core, it's the ability to take a pulse on the current situation in which you find yourself.

Those who can read the room recognize the specific people in it, assess the vibe, and then choose actions based on those observations. It might be the overall office mood, a specific internal meeting, or a sales call with a customer, yet the lesson applies similarly and can be summed up in this very scientific equation:

Be aware of yourself
+
Be aware of others
=
Act accordingly

I'm confident that these two tales will paint the picture clearly enough, so without further ado we'll jump right into our opening act of Steakhouse Snafu and end with the headliner, Sales Meeting Foot-in-Mouth.

A large group from our company had just arrived in a Midwestern city for an annual industry convention. Our kickoff dinner for the week took place at a higher-end steakhouse. There were approximately 40 of us in a reserved section, with two long tables of 20 for our group. I was seated diagonally from our VP of Sales, our highest-ranking official at this dinner, and next to my regional manager as well.

When the bill was delivered to our table, I saw our VP lower his glasses from the top of his head down to the tip of his nose with a look of concern. I remember thinking that he was likely taking a moment to absorb the rather large sum that 40 entrees plus multiple sides and drinks amounted to. As we would soon learn, I had mistaken the specific source of his concern.

As he glanced up with a stern look, he exclaimed in his distinct East Coast accent, "Who ordered the lobstah?" Things just got interesting.

Soon we would learn that most of our colleagues ordered steak entrées, which were $40-$45 each, except for two people. Instead, they felt like it was a good idea to order the fresh lobster tail, by far the most expensive item on the menu at $125 per plate.

To make matters worse, they were new to the company, having just started the previous month. This was not a good first impression to make at dinner with their new boss or their boss's boss, our suddenly irked VP.

When in doubt, it's best to observe and adapt, especially in a relatively neutral situation such as a work dinner.

In a scenario like this, inquire with those around you or just take a moment to observe and listen to what people are ordering. If you don't want steak, then order chicken or pork. If you don't eat meat, try the pasta. There were so many better options than ordering *by far* the priciest option on the menu and subsequently standing out like a sore thumb.

Hopefully this first example is somewhat relatable and highlights the importance of observing those around you and utilizing some common sense. Our second story, the Foot-in-Mouth, trades the steakhouse for a sales meeting and reinforces the importance of both self-awareness and being aware of others.

The event was our national sales meeting, and the ambiance was the standard magical setting for such an occasion: a large, dimly lit, windowless hotel conference room. At this particular meeting, we were learning about annual growth targets in relation to sales quotas for the new fiscal year, a subject of significant interest to most sales reps.

The quota reveal is an annual staple in the life of a sales rep, and our company at the time normally set the quotas in the 6-8% growth range. However, this year the powers that be decided that we needed to grow more, and a larger increase to 12% was announced. The overall reaction was one of surprise and concern, as whispers began to build in small pockets around the room. However, a large meeting in front of all your coworkers is usually not the best spot to stand up and register a formal complaint.

In order to relate the specificity of this next part of the story, a quick explanation of our territory sizes at the time is required. The smallest territories were in the annual revenue range of $2 million, and the largest ones were around $5 million. Each territory has a similar number of potential customers and sales opportunities, yet some territories grew over time and others declined, which accounts for the wide gap in the ranges of revenue.

A quick trip to the calculator shows that 12% of a $5 million territory is a whopping $600,000 in required revenue growth. In contrast, a 12% revenue growth on a $2 million territory is a smaller and more manageable $240,000 for the year. If anyone should have had a logical and legitimate gripe about the impact of our shiny new 12% quota, it would have been the reps with the larger territories. However, that's not how it all went down.

Of all our 32 sales reps, the first and only person who stood up to complain immediately caught our attention, as it wasn't a rep from one of the larger territories. On the contrary, it was a rep who carried a quota of about $2.1 million, the *smallest* territory by revenue in the entire company.

The audacity of this rep beamed brightly that day. Those of us with larger territories now had to grow $500,000 to $600,000 compared to his $240,000, and yet *he* stood up to complain about a growth number less than half of ours? Every single territory sales rep other than him has to grow more in revenue than he does, yet he's the one publicly pleading for mercy. His vocal position certainly didn't land well with most, and garnered little empathy from his coworkers. He did not think that through, and he certainly did not read the room effectively at all.

In a twist of irony, his complaint was partially responsible for helping large territory reps and hurting small territory ones. Over the next 12 months, management agreed that the larger territories *should* have a lower percentage growth goal than the smaller ones.

The logic made sense, as larger territories have already grown their business effectively and smaller territories have much more business yet to win. From then on, in the example of an 8%

company growth goal, smaller territories would have to grow 10% while larger ones would only have to grow about 6%.

That concludes our story time about reading the room. Hopefully one or both of those tales connected and gave some insight into the importance of being self-aware in the corporate world, in addition to being aware of others and your surroundings. As you continue to build this skill, it should help prevent missteps and present more opportunities to succeed.

JERKS, PHONIES, AND PEOPLE FROM NEW YORK

THE MORE TIME we spend in the corporate world, the better we should become at observing our surroundings, which of course includes colleagues and customers. Corporate America is full of all kinds of people with all kinds of attitudes and personalities.

At your company there will be excellent colleagues who bring positivity and wisdom to the workplace, and even become extended members of your social circle. Unfortunately, you may also work alongside some disrespectful and downright rude people. Others will just be flat-out fake.

Three different kinds of people you will encounter in the corporate world are jerks, phonies, and people from New York. It will be difficult to avoid the jerks and phonies entirely, but it will be helpful to identify all three and act accordingly.

> *Watch out for jerks and phonies, and listen to people from New York. If executed correctly, I'm confident this can provide positive outcomes.*

Let's begin with New Yorkers and the Northeast as a whole, since this portion is a little more playful and the other two will carry the negative weight for this lesson. Yes, that means putting a positive spin on people from the Northeast, not a pessimistic one.

For the purposes of this lesson, I'm speaking geographically of an area that stretches somewhere from Philadelphia and New Jersey all the way up through New York and Boston. Although I'm painting with a broad brush here, the canvas generally shows that people from the Northeast are more candid and direct. Multiple experiences with colleagues and customers over the last 20 years have shown this to be accurate.

For whatever reason, Northeast natives tend to tell it like it is with very little sugarcoating. On the surface, this quality seems like it could be abrasive and offensive in the corporate world. Indeed, it can backfire or create unnecessary conflict when applied too aggressively, but there's also a positive way to look at being candid and direct.

When looking for genuine, quality feedback, we usually can't do much better than a Northeasterner. Similar to seeking advice from anyone in your personal life, of course you want to make sure the advisor is of sound mind. So yes, a level-headed and intelligent person from the Northeast is often our ideal source for feedback.

As a Midwest native and resident, the forthright Northeast approach was initially a little off-putting. However, over time it grew on me as a beneficial opportunity to obtain transparent feedback about anything from the performance of a product to the effectiveness of your customer care team. It feels like politeness is the natural human reaction, but the Northeast approach of candor and tough love can break down barriers and help spur progress or improvement in business.

The next two aren't so rosy, as we transition to the more negative portion of this lesson with phonies and jerks. There are plenty of them scattered across the corporate landscape, and I'm guessing in many other places of employment as well.

Encountering jerks and phonies in the workplace is a little different than in our personal lives. If we meet rude, arrogant people or those who appear to be fake in a social setting, we usually have the choice to not associate with them in the future. Unless of course it's the good friend of our significant other. In that case, we're all stuck!

At work we are often forced to interact with phonies and jerks on a regular basis, and that can be a frustrating exercise. Identifying them is the first step, and that is of course another area in which reading the room can prove to be beneficial.

I'm not sure there is a structured or detailed strategy for dealing with these difficult kinds of people at work, other than exercising restraint. Over time, both phonies and jerks usually reveal themselves in unflattering fashion for everyone to see. It's far more advantageous to let a colleague show their true negative colors to coworkers than for you to try and shine a light on it. Therefore, what has seemed to work best over time is a simple and basic approach consisting of two principles: patience and kindness.

Jerks don't usually utilize patience or kindness at work, so the natural human reaction might be to respond with similar levels of impatience and abrasiveness. Don't fall for that approach. Jerks often push even harder to win battles when faced with their own brand of rudeness and impatience. Instead, I suggest killing them with kindness. At the very least, you can balance and neutralize their approach, and at the most you might actually begin to win them over, which can be beneficial especially if they are above you on the corporate ladder.

Phonies are a different entity altogether; in most cases they are not willing to be genuine or show any evidence of their true persona. They exist at most companies and they are difficult to connect with on a professional or personal level.

We still have to interact with phonies to complete our work

efficiently since we can't just flat-out ignore them. However, they can be wolves in sheep's clothing, so be amicable and only interact with them as much as required to still accomplish your job.

It would be great if there was some kind of magic wand that we could wave and solve the annoyance of phonies and jerks in the workplace. Exercising patience and kindness might not be the perfect approach, but I'm confident that it will help more times than it hurts.

THE RULE OF THREE

O N YOUR MARK, get set, go. Goldilocks and the Three Bears. Life, liberty, and the pursuit of happiness.

The Rule of Three is indeed a concept that appears across multiple venues in society. Whether it's starting a race, storytelling, or the formation of our country, examples of its use can be found and analyzed across many different applications.

It's a strategy that can help people explain and present clear messaging in both their professional and personal lives. For our purposes, I will narrow that focus to the corporate landscape and how it can benefit everything from internal presentations to external sales pitches.

Presenting information in groups of three is more memorable and effective at connecting with people. Humans are accustomed to patterns in threes and thus find them appealing and easy to process.

The Rule of Three is a valuable resource for sales reps, and can also be useful in everything from pitching a marketing campaign to engineers explaining difficult concepts to coworkers. If there is a subset of material or concepts that needs to be conveyed, or taught by one group and learned by another, the Rule of Three can usually help and rarely harms the process. This is probably one of the areas of the book that can help well beyond the corporate world, especially in teaching classroom topics to students in school.

The Rule of Three narrows the scope and focuses on the three most important takeaways, making the message clearer and more palatable for the intended audience.

I learned this concept early on in my corporate career from my sales mentor Jon, and it helped me immensely. The primary use for the Rule of Three in a sales role is to assure we keep things simple, focused, and appealing for the customer. If we're going into their office with a new solution to sell, we want to keep them engaged in the process and aligned with our ultimate goal. Connecting with how the human brain best processes and absorbs content is most definitely in a sales rep's best interest.

Whether it's for sales calls with customers or internal presentations at your company, try to cap it at a limit of three key points for any individual meeting or topic. If there is too much content or too many different topics to simplify it down to three, you're probably better off scheduling a second meeting or follow-up call. Two short presentations that connect and resonate are better than one long, unorganized presentation that is too content-heavy and loses or confuses the customer.

Other departments can benefit from the Rule of Three as well. Everything from pitching a marketing campaign to presenting data-heavy engineering topics can utilize this narrowed scope. Human resources can highlight the three most unique benefits or reasons to come work for a company. Financial topics can seem like a foreign language to non-financial minds, so boil it down to three and try to keep it simple.

I have witnessed many excellent and memorable presentations over a span of 20 years, providing a clear and coherent experience for the audience. Unfortunately, I have also labored through dumpster fires that were either organized poorly or delivered with little direction or definition. Utilizing the Rule of Three can help extinguish these fires or prevent them from starting in the first place.

One of my least favorite sights at the beginning of a presentation is when the content overview slide contains something like 11 different topics, each with their own bold bullet point staring back at me. Some presenters forget that the human brain usually cringes at a long list of new items that will be covered and presumably required to learn or at least recall.

Others think it's a good idea to write way too much on each of their slides and read continuously from them in one long-winded delivery. When in doubt, the fewer words the better on a slide, as it facilitates presenting to the audience as opposed to reading to them. Instead of ambiguous ramblings, focus on three specific areas to help align with the audience and the natural preferences of our brains.

I once sat through an internal presentation that was memorable for all the wrong reasons. The PowerPoint slides included full sentences and paragraphs, forming one sloppy run-on thought with little focus. The presenter then proceeded to essentially turn and read from the screen the rest of the way, resulting in an uninspiring presentation and a pretty tough watch.

Nearly every role in the corporate world will require employees to present concepts or ideas at some point. Take the time to prepare and practice for presentations and speeches in addition to utilizing the Rule of Three. The benefits are felt by the audience and will help presenters accomplish their goals.

.

REMOTE CONTROL

WORKING FROM THE office five days a week had been the standard expectation for the entire existence of corporations. However, all of that changed in 2020. The years since then have been an awkward balancing act between work from office and work from home.

Prior to the pandemic, remote work from an employee's home was a rare perk. A handful of corporate roles such as field marketing manager, sales rep, and service technician have traditionally required workers to spend a majority of their time out in the field away from the office. Beyond that, most employees were bound to the cubicle for at least four and usually all five days of the workweek.

The uncertainty of the pandemic ushered in the modern era of remote work flexibility and hybrid roles for many jobs that were traditionally office-based. Along with that came a set of both acceptable and unacceptable protocols for workers, not to mention a slew of new headaches for corporate management to deal with from a distance.

Working from home can be both a productive blessing and a seductive curse. Manage it appropriately, and you'll end up with the former instead of the latter.

While the debate lives on regarding productivity and sustainability, remote work and the flexibility to work from home in some capacity appear here to stay. Following the Rule of Three, the keys to maximizing productivity and fostering a positive experience working from home are: Develop a Routine, Minimize Distractions, and Get Out.

1. Develop a Routine

One of the keys to successful remote work is to develop a consistent routine. Try to wake up and start work at the same time every day, even if your first call or virtual meeting isn't until mid-morning. If your first scheduled call isn't until 10 in the morning, that's not an excuse to crack the laptop open at 9:45.

Select a specific time – maybe it's 8 or 8:30 – to mentally arrive at the home office and begin the day from your residential workstation. Plan your pre-work routine and specific wake-up time from there, whether you require an A.M. trip to the gym or are more of a "wake up ready to go" kind of person.

Remember that being on camera is either required or strongly suggested at most companies, so be ready to look presentable (at least on the top half!) by making time to shower or eliminate any bedhead disasters. No hats or hooded sweatshirts, either – it's simply unprofessional. As a rule of thumb, dress business casual on top at home the same way you would for the office. Comfy shorts or flannel pants that wouldn't be acceptable in the office are one perk of working from home, as they won't be seen on camera.

Prioritize your workday based on what tasks are most important to complete that day or week, and manage that time accordingly around your scheduled meetings and calls. It can help to keep a notepad handy and track two fluid lists: tasks that need to be completed this week, and tasks that need to be completed today. There are likely multiple items on each list, and this can help stay on point and also keep you in good standing with your manager.

Developing a consistent routine is good practice whether working in an office cubicle or at a desk from home. It carries even more weight virtually because when working from home, there are significantly more distractions that can pull your eyes and attention away from work.

2. Minimize Distractions

Working from home is a privilege, not a right. If your company has a remote-first or hybrid work policy, they are trusting you to perform your role away from the office. They are also paying you the same amount as an office-first job, and as an extra bonus, remote work deposits several hours of commute time (plus gas or transportation money) back on your side.

Treat the privilege with due respect. Don't form distracting habits like doing house chores during the core workday. One quick load of laundry here or there, and all of a sudden you're doing the dishes and cleaning the bathroom during the gap between your afternoon calls. The same goes for a midday trip to the grocery store, or trying to take advantage of reduced crowds at the gym in the early afternoon.

Avoid these contagious midday traps as much as possible. Just because you can doesn't mean you should, so keep those bad habits at bay.

Admittedly, I can relate from experience since I let myself get off track one winter a few years back and thankfully was able to nip it in the bud. I grew to despise leaving the house after work during the cold days of winter when it gets dark out before 5. There's plenty of time to get personal necessities done outside of the core workday. We did it before the pandemic, and we can do it again even when working remotely full time.

In between scheduled phone calls and virtual meetings, be sure to work on completing your tasks instead of filling that time with chores or other activities. However, we should not stay affixed to the home workstation all day long, as feeling locked up inside all day can grow into a legit concern. It can sneak up quickly, especially since the traditional noon lunch hour is difficult to preserve when company-wide remote work stretches over four time zones vying for open space in Outlook calendars. So make sure to take a break.

3. Get Out.

Do not let your work laptop and company phone suck you into a continuous nine-hour vortex every single weekday, especially when working from home. The intangible boundary between residence and office can become easily blurred with full-time or even part-time remote work.

During core work hours, make sure to take brief breaks and leave home as well. Select a day or two each week to work from a local coffee shop for a couple hours to complete some laptop-based tasks. Schedule a 15-minute walk for some fresh air in the early afternoon after lunch. During the warmer seasons, try taking your remote workspace to a picnic table at a park or somewhere with Wi-Fi access and work outside for an hour between calls.

These are all acceptable forms of getting out of the house while working virtually and should be implemented to help keep a level head while balancing work from home with live from home. Just be cautious not to let them morph into distractions.

Another important facet of getting out and managing the remote workday is making sure it doesn't leak into weekday evenings. One suggestion for those who have a dedicated work phone is to place it out of sight after 5:30 or 6 P.M. Try not to look at it again until 8 the next morning. This practice can help establish boundaries and keep work from infringing on everything from dinner to weeknight personal time.

Additionally, if your company's work policy is remote-first and you happen to be within commuting distance of the office, go in and work for a couple days a month even if it's not required.

Align with a few coworkers willing to do the same and then grab lunch with them at a nearby restaurant. You may even impress management, who could be there that day and still value employee collaboration at the office even when it's not mandated.

In the modern corporate world, many traditional office-based jobs can be performed remotely for much of the time as long as they are supplemented with in-person events. Meetings that physically gather everyone together are both necessary and beneficial, as there is no equivalent substitute for those. Hopefully your company recognizes that and acts accordingly.

Any onboarding program for new hires should be conducted live at the office as well, ideally with other colleagues in attendance. I can't imagine remote onboarding being a healthy start to learning a company and absorbing its culture, especially for a new hire out of college.

Most roles and responsibilities beyond the onboarding period can then be accomplished working remotely.

THE INTERVIEW

THE BACK OF the book may seem like an odd spot for the lesson on interviews, yet there is a valid reason behind it.

An argument could be made for placing it near the beginning, as job interviews clearly precede job offers and starting your initial role in the workforce. I chose this location on the basis that many readers will have already gone through interviews, secured their job, and perhaps even begun working. My hope is that for anyone who doesn't need the information in this chapter, scanning or skipping it here toward the end of the book will have less impact on the overall reading experience.

With that in mind, this chapter features a brief and limited lesson for the simple fact that there are tens and maybe hundreds of existing resources that help graduates prepare for their interviews. Everything from what to do before, how to dress during, and when to follow up after are covered extensively. In a mild violation of the Rule of Three, there are two key takeaways for those who are still going through the interview process.

Prepare and smile. Take the time to practice both, and it will help your cause.

Let's start with the obvious one, which is preparation. Take the time in advance of your interviews to research the company and the specific role. Spend a few minutes on their website and social media accounts to get a good feel for their business and their culture. Continue the exploration beyond the company resources and learn about the industry and any current developments or trends.

If you want to potentially impress an HR recruiter or a hiring manager, prepare a specific question or two pertaining to these company and industry findings. "I noticed the company recently launched a new technology that isn't available from your primary competitors. Is that accurate and, if so, how is it impacting your business so far?"

Another good strategy is to put yourself in the shoes of a current employee, thinking back to their onboarding period and first few months with the company. Something along the lines of, "What do you think is the one piece of advice that current people in this role would give to a new hire starting the position?"

These are examples of insightful, open-ended questions that inspire thought specifically from hiring managers. They much prefer these kinds of questions that show an employee took time to prepare and conduct research, as opposed to simple or dull ones that could have been pulled or composed just from reading the description in the job posting.

Our second suggestion might be viewed as corny and uncomfortable. Well, first interviews out of college *can* be uncomfortable, so it should be good practice.

Make sure to smile in your interview, especially when you're talking. Not the entire time like a deranged clown – just a calm and confident smile. How do we practice and achieve this? By talking into a mirror and smiling.

Yep, I said it. Just give it a try by reading a random article, a couple paragraphs from the company website, or even your personal elevator speech into a mirror. Yes, you should have a brief personal elevator speech, preparing an answer to the question, "Why should we hire you?" Read it once out loud into the mirror without smiling, and then repeat it while smiling a comfortable and non-clown amount.

If you conduct this experiment and don't notice a difference, then this exercise might not be for you, and that's okay. However, I'm confident you'll see a positive energy upgrade with the smiling approach, and that your potential future manager will too.

Additionally, find your happy place right before the interview. Play some of your favorite upbeat hot jams before walking into the interview. Watch a funny video online or a quick clip of a stand-up comedian that you know will get you smiling or laughing. I'm confident that finding your happy place has the ability to translate into positive vibes during your interview, and I doubt it can hurt.

DOWN THE CORPORATE HIGHWAY

The Shelf Life of a Diploma

UP UNTIL THIS point of the book, I have relayed several observations and lessons that can be applied when entering the workforce. My primary goal is to provide a resource that informs and prepares for year one in the corporate world.

Hopefully we have built an effective corporate burrito to bring to your first job, or if you have already started your new role, simply added some guac.

Now it's time for a brief look beyond the first year, providing some advice in certain areas you may encounter a little further down the road.

For starters, let's begin with your college diploma. It certainly has more longevity than fresh meat or produce. It's more like a box of pasta or rice that can sit in the cabinet and be pulled out at a moment's notice. However, a diploma will slowly lose its freshness and relevance over time.

> *Your college diploma has a shelf life. Make sure to consume it before it grows stale.*

A diploma from a specific college or university is a relevant resource to utilize beyond graduation, and it generally consists of three components.

First, the education itself. Four years of higher learning with a specific focus on your major's core content are hopefully in line with the specific companies and positions to which you apply.

If not, that's okay too; there are several reasons why an educational exploration can veer off course. It could be a random class that sparked a new interest, an "aha moment" at an internship, or an inspiring experience from your personal life. If that's the case, just make sure to have a good story to explain how your major focus has taken a minor detour.

The second postgraduate application for your diploma is networking and job hunting. Many universities conduct alumni events within an extended area of campus as well as in major markets around the country.

Employed graduates from certain colleges have been known to curry favor toward fellow alumni, so connect with as many alumni as you can. Take advantage of these opportunities throughout your 20s, as that's when your diploma is still fresh.

The third part is the fun one, the social component. That consists of everything from staying in touch with friends from your freshman dorm all the way to adult alumni trips and reunions. The long-term social aspects will of course vary among different universities and circles of friends, but it's a unique bond that is difficult to replicate in other areas of life.

I am a proud graduate of Marquette University in Milwaukee, and please forgive the brief personal story to help convey an example of the fun social component. Every year after graduation, a group of friends the year behind me in school organized an annual Saturday bus trip from Chicago to Milwaukee for a Marquette basketball game. I was fortunate to join up with this event a few trips into its existence. It was always a full day of nostalgic fun and even provided the chance to meet new alumni and friends of friends as well.

The bus trip was a highlight on the calendar each winter. Over time, the reality of jobs, families, and weekend activities set in, and now some years the trip either takes place in a reduced form or gets skipped. Through no fault of anyone, especially its core organizers who crushed it every year, it's a legit challenge to keep that kind of weekend excursion going consistently into our 30s and 40s. Events such as these are tough to maintain long-term, so treasure these special times while you can.

The primary takeaway is to maximize the college experience and the diploma in your postgraduate years. At some point in your 20s, the companies and the roles in which you work will take precedence over your specific degree and the areas you studied in school.

Hopefully your diploma and the entire college experience are a combination of valued resources and fond memories. The professional applications can be especially beneficial to alumni in their 20s, yet they will begin to show their shelf life through the years. The social ones are a little more variable, sometimes lasting into our 30s or 40s and can occasionally last a lifetime for the fortunate ones.

PASSION VS. PROFESSION

A S THE MONTHS turn to years and eventually a decade or two, it's common for the comfort of your steady job and paycheck to slowly morph into frustration and disdain. The passion, engagement, or drive to succeed for you and your company can begin to unravel and wither over time.

In reality, the monotony of the recurring work week can take its toll, especially one that entails reporting to the same office every single day. The five-day weeks and 52-week fiscal years can congeal and blend together, which can negatively affect a person's attitude and disposition.

As a whole, the corporate world is a good way to make a decent or even lucrative living, yet, like many jobs, it can be a grind over the long haul. If we're not careful, it can wear away at our energy, positivity, and passion.

The good news is that we can proactively separate profession from passion, preserving our energy and livelihood in its more natural habitat: our personal lives.

We don't have to be passionate about our specific jobs, the companies we work for, or even our careers.

Keep profession separate from passion, and prevent work from infiltrating the other areas of your life.

The most important factor in passion preservation is to recognize that it's perfectly acceptable for work to be nothing more than a source of income for survival and livelihood. As we get a few years under our belts, perhaps with a promotion and some additional responsibility, it's easy to get caught up in corporate life and idly watch its presence intrude into our personal lives. Be watchful for signs of that, and try your best to proactively confine work into the core weekday business hours.

Our work doesn't have to be some significant, elaborate career that positively impacts society or defines your existence. Of course, we all still have to show up to work and perform our jobs to certain standards, but it doesn't have to engulf our personal lives or eliminate our hobbies and passions.

Once we recognize this fact, we can begin to plan accordingly and put thought into action. Start by making a list of the hobbies or activities that you have done or still want to do on weekdays.

Has an expanded role at work caused you to contemplate leaving your friends' Tuesday night softball league or Thursday night basketball game? Don't give it up – keep playing. Does the local bar's trivia night keep calling your obnoxiously clever team name? Keep going to it every week you can. It's great to have fun at recurring events that help break up the week.

Perhaps you've even thought about taking a passion for something like arts and crafts to a slightly higher level, creating items for friends or even exploring selling to others. Schedule an hour or two for it at least one weeknight per week and maintain its place in your life. Once we stop playing on teams with friends or making time for our favorite hobbies, a little bit of what makes us a unique or vibrant individual can start to drift away.

Too often, society tries to define who we are by our job or career. Try not to let that happen. If you maintain your passion and independence while keeping a rational balance between work time and personal time, you are more likely to enjoy both at a higher level. This spot may seem like a logical time to use the phrase "work-life balance." However, it has become an overused cliché in corporate circles. Finding a fair split between our work and personal lives has almost become table stakes these days, as it's often recognized by companies across the corporate landscape. My advice is not to use that phrase at work.

If you're fortunate enough in life to build some kind of legacy down the road and be revered by those around you, it will likely be for things within your circle of family and friends, not with work. A fun and caring friend, a supportive sibling, a loving parent, or a valued member of the community in which you live.

Want to know one scenario that we rarely see? "My dad is my rock. He's my biggest advocate and has supported me through failures and coached me to success. But forget about all that – you should see the way he coaches his team of employees at work. He should have his own statue there!"

Here's another one you're not likely to hear: "Hey, you know my friend Olivia? She's fun to hang out with on weekends, she's there for me during the tough times, and she makes a killer margarita too! But what's even more impressive is her killer spreadsheets and the way she crunches numbers downtown as a financial analyst!"

There is a pretty fair yet often unspoken agreement in the corporate world. Most salaried employees are expected to provide 40 to 50 hours of work around the core set of weekday business hours. In exchange, they should be permitted freedom on most weeknights and weekends. Of course, there will be the occasional dinner with customers or a convention that requires travel – just make sure it stays the exception and doesn't slowly morph into the rule.

It won't always be easy, but the effort to compartmentalize your professional and personal worlds and keep your passions alive is a worthy cause. The hobbies, sports, and activities that you loved playing in high school and continued playing in college should not fall victim to the corporate world.

NEVER FALL IN LOVE WITH A COMPANY

I'T'S TIME FOR a short but sweet lesson, one that is as genuine as any other in the book. I also can't fathom a situation in the future where this observation begins to reverse itself, so I'm confident we can carve this lesson into wet cement.

Never fall in love with a company.
A person can love you back;
a company cannot.

This statement is another gem I learned from my dad. There are countless examples of its validity from my 20+ years in the corporate world, and I'm guessing from others at this level of experience and beyond.

At some point in your career, you may find yourself ready to exclaim, "I love this company! I would do anything for it." You may even hear coworkers say it.

I have heard it, and admittedly I even felt it and said it once. I was wrong. If you feel it rising or hear it verbalized, I strongly recommend that you hit the pause button. Recognize its flawed logic, then reframe the thoughts about this situation that has created a false sense of love.

Think about the people and pets you love. There is a living, breathing person or a cuddly canine on the other side of that emotional equation, one who also has feelings and can love you back.

Companies are simply not capable of anything that resembles loving a person back. They are inherently built to make tough bottom-line decisions that can result in employees being treated as line items on a spreadsheet. I have been in closed-door discussions that literally assess people as a number and a salary amount, utilizing factors such as operating expenses and role redundancy to determine whether a person makes the cut or gets cut.

At its core, the dynamic between company and employee is a transactional relationship. Companies define a role and pay workers for it; those workers in return perform the role and collect the payments.

The fortunate ones in the corporate world are those who work for excellent leaders and with great people. They are likely a combination of talented, hardworking, intelligent, respectful, and fun. Make no mistake, it is human quality and capital that lead companies to success, and on the flip side it's often the people whose questionable demeanor and poor decisions cause companies to fail.

It's okay to respect and like a coworker or manager, and in some cases it can border on feelings of love. That's the people side of things, and it's even healthy to a certain extent. There is no such thing as company-employee love in the corporate world, so make sure to never fall in love with a company.

Out on a High Note

I T WILL HAPPEN to almost every single occupant of the corporate world. At some point, you will likely leave your current company for a new and exciting opportunity somewhere else.

You may have found the new role through a networking connection or industry recruiter, a family member or friend. Perhaps you just got to the point where you simply needed a fresh start and found it via your own online job hunt. When the time comes to exit, do it the right way.

> **Leave the company with the theoretical idea that you'll be returning someday. Plant some seeds before you cross the bridge, and don't set that bridge ablaze on your way out.**

First and foremost, plan accordingly to provide your manager with two weeks' notice. It's expected and is also the respectful thing to do. Deliver this message in person, or on a phone call if in person is not an option.

Do not do it over email or text. It's a significant moment that deserves a discussion, and anything less than two weeks also makes your manager's job much more difficult. The spoken notice will also allow you to control the message with gratitude and class, thanking your manager for the opportunity to work on their team and learn from them.

Thank your colleagues as well for the time spent together and any specific things you learned from them. Sometimes this can only be accomplished on a large scale by email or Slack, and that's okay.

Customize them and send individual messages of gratitude, avoiding the cringeworthy high school yearbook style of "Thanks for the great times, everyone! I'll miss you and let's keep in touch!" If you do have a close colleague or mentor at this company, that could warrant a more personalized interaction such as a phone call or in-person meeting.

It's up to you how you exit the company, but try to leave a positive impact and the door slightly ajar for the opportunity to someday come back. It may never come to fruition, and the circumstances that drove you to leave in the first place will make it seem unlikely in the moment. However, I did find myself in this situation, and it paid off like I never could have imagined.

After seven years with my first company, a new opportunity came calling in a similar yet different industry. I was not going to work for a direct competitor, so the standard two weeks' notice was accepted. Then I decided to go a little overboard, or at least it seemed so at the time. It's difficult to tell this story without patting my own back a little, so apologies for the boasting manner in which this may come across.

My manager Kevin was the one who hired me at the start. He aligned me with a great sales rep and my mentor, Jon. Kevin also promoted me, and he deserved to realize my gratitude for that. I purchased a gift card to an upscale local restaurant that I knew he and his wife enjoyed, and made sure it was enough for two people to wine and dine comfortably without spending a dollar of their own.

As a field sales rep, the customer care team can often make or break your accounts' experience doing business with the company. It's a largely thankless and commission-free job, so I decided to send our support team a large gift basket full of gourmet cookies and brownies. Our core team and their manager thanked me and said they couldn't remember ever receiving a gift like this from someone leaving the company.

If I recall, the entire amount spent on both items was about $300. I'm not sure of the accurate way to calculate the payoff on that futures wager, but the total amount added a couple more zeros. Long story short, my new opportunity did not work out as planned. I kept in touch with Kevin and Jon, and one year later there was an opportunity to come back and rejoin the company and the team that I left a mere 12 months ago. Since that moment, I have worked together with them for *nine* additional years at two companies, largely due to a graceful exit.

If your next opportunity is taking you to a new company, be sure to leave your current one in good standing. In our personal lives and in the professional world, we simply can't predict what's waiting for us around the corner.

Afterword

I HOPE WE ACCOMPLISHED the three primary goals to inform, prepare, and entertain. I'm confident that if you implement a few of the lessons, especially any particular ones that resonate strongly, it will help set the table for success during your rookie year in the workforce.

I hope to continue the reach of this pamphlet-on-steroids that they let me call a book. My goal is to speak to graduating seniors and business classes at universities, as well as corporations that hire college grads for entry-level roles.

Part of this effort is underway, as I've begun working with universities in the Midwest to incorporate the content into their coursework.

Lastly, please allow me to introduce you to Second Serve Creations. Second Serve is the imprint under which this book is published. I'm excited to explore how this entity will develop and evolve in the long term; for now I'm referring to it simply as a Creation Station.

The initial focus will contain three specific areas:

1. Keep on writing and continue to publish

2. Provide a resource for aspiring writers

3. Give back and help others

Second Serve will feature books, and I'm using the plural form with cautious optimism. A new idea is currently in development and will hopefully become the next publication, with others to follow alongside the university and corporate opportunities.

The next goal is to provide some kind of creative and educational outlet for aspiring writers. Navigating the formal publishing process for the first time can be a confusing journey – at least it was for me. I would enjoy the opportunity to pay it forward and assist other publishing rookies in the future. For starters, I am journaling the publishing process from start to finish, with the intent of providing it as a reference for writers during their initial publishing effort.

The third initiative is to give back and help others. Second Serve is a reference to tennis, a sport I have grown to love playing in recent years. Tennis is unique: It requires athleticism and skill, it can be played well into our 60s and 70s, and every serve gets a second chance. With the inclusion of a second serve in tennis, I like to think that the sport's inventor, Major Walter Clopton Wingfield (what a name!) appreciated second chances.

Our goal within Second Serve is to celebrate second chances in life, and we will be donating to causes that support second chances in both our personal and professional lives. The first organization that we will contribute to is NAMI, the National Alliance on Mental Illness. We will be donating 10% of all profits from the sale of this book to NAMI. More about this story and its origin can be found online at Secondservecreations. com, so we invite you to visit and check it out.

For consulting or speaking inquiries with
universities and corporations,
please contact me at
kevin@secondservecreations.com.

ACKNOWLEDGMENTS

SPECIAL THANKS TO Joel, Laura, Sayde, and the entire team at Launch My Book. Your knowledge and talent turned this rough manuscript into an actual publication, guiding me through the entire process.

Thank you is hardly enough, and I look forward to the opportunity to work together on future creations.

About the Author

Writing is one of my passions.

Make no mistake, it is not my career . . . yet. Twenty years at five different companies holding roles in Sales and Project Management is how I've been able to pay the bills and live an enjoyable life.

It was a coincidence the first time I got bit by the writing bug, and frankly I did not have the purest of intentions. As a high school freshman, a couple friends and I were discussing what courses to enroll in for sophomore year. Our friend Paul had secured some insider info from a current sophomore that was of particular interest. He had learned about the existence of a rare species of educational experience: the blow-off class.

It was Intro to Journalism, and with sincere apologies to its excellent and witty teacher, Mrs. Levin, the course description floating around the school hallways seemed too good to be true:

Intro to Journalism (Hallway Version)

- Learn how to write better
- Create some articles for the school newspaper
- No tests! Grades are assigned based on those articles
- Course prerequisite: willingness to leave the classroom to "explore your creative space" (visit the school's main hangout area outside the cafeteria for extended periods of time).

I made a decision: This white whale had to be caught. Blow-off or not, I started to develop a passion for writing. After 20+ years spent in the corporate world, I'm happy to state that passion still exists, and hopefully there is still more writing to come in my future.

secondservecreations.com

Notes